Kingdom
POLITICS

GOVERNMENT *from*
GOD'S PERSPECTIVE

TONY EVANS

Lifeway Press®
Brentwood, Tennessee

Editorial Team

Heather Hair
Writer

Tyler Quillet
Managing Editor

Reid Patton
Senior Editor

Joel Polk
Publisher & *Manager, Adult Discipleship*

Stephanie Cross
Assoicate Editor

John Paul Basham
Director, Lifeway Adult Publishing

Jon Rodda
Art Director

Published by Lifeway Press® • © 2024 Tony Evans

ISBN: 978-1-4300-8526-3

Item number: 005846087

Dewey decimal classification: 261.7
Subject heading: CHRISTIANITY AND POLITICS \ CHURCH AND STATE \ RELIGION AND POLITICS

My deepest thanks go to Mrs. Heather Hair for her skills and insights in collaboration on this manuscript.

Scripture quotations taken from the (NASB®) New American Standard Bible®, Copyright © 1960, 1971, 1977, 1995, 2020 by The Lockman Foundation. Used by permission. All rights reserved. www.lockman.org

To order additional copies of this resource, write to Lifeway Resources Customer Service; 200 Powell Place, Suite 100; Brentwood, TN 37027-7707; fax 615-251-5933; call toll free 800-458-2772; order online at lifeway.com; email orderentry@lifeway.com.

Printed in the United States of America

Adult Ministry Publishing • Lifeway Resources
200 Powell Place, Suite 100 • Brentwood, TN 37027-7707

Contents

About the Author

Dr. Tony Evans is the founder and senior pastor of Oak Cliff Bible Fellowship in Dallas, founder and president of The Urban Alternative, former chaplain of the NBA's Dallas Mavericks, and author of over one hundred books, booklets, and Bible studies. The first African American to earn a doctorate of theology from Dallas Theological Seminary, he has been named one of the twelve most effective preachers in the English-speaking world by Baylor University. Dr. Evans holds the honor of writing and publishing the first full-Bible commentary and study Bible by an African American.

His radio broadcast, *The Alternative* with Dr. Tony Evans, can be heard on more than 1,400 US outlets daily and in more than 130 countries.

Dr. Evans launched the Tony Evans Training Center in 2017, an online learning platform providing quality seminary-style courses for a fraction of the cost to any person in any place. The goal is to increase Bible literacy not only in lay people but also in those Christian leaders who cannot afford or find the time for formal ongoing education.

Dr. Tony Evans was married to his late wife, Lois, for nearly fifty years. They are the proud parents of four, grandparents of thirteen, and great-grandparents of three.

For more information, visit TonyEvans.org.

How to Get the Most from This Study

This Bible study book includes six weeks of content for group and personal study.

Group Sessions

Regardless of what day of the week your group meets, each week of content begins with the group session. Each group session uses the following format to facilitate meaningful interaction among group members, with God's Word, and with the teaching of Dr. Evans.

START. This page includes questions to get the conversation started and to introduce the video teaching.

WATCH. This page includes key points from Dr. Evans's teaching, along with blanks for taking notes as participants watch the video.

DISCUSS. This page includes questions and statements that guide the group to respond to Dr. Evans's video teaching and to relevant Bible passages.

Personal Study

Each week provides three days of personal study and learning activities for individual engagement between group sessions: "Hit the Streets" and two Bible studies.

HIT THE STREETS. This section highlights practical steps for taking the week's teaching and putting it into practice.

BIBLE STUDIES. These personal studies revisit stories, Scriptures, and themes introduced in the videos to help participants understand and apply them on a personal level.

Tips for Leading a Small Group

Follow these guidelines to prepare for each group session.

Prayerfully Prepare

REVIEW. Review the weekly material and group questions ahead of time.

PRAY. Be intentional about praying for each person in the group.

Ask the Holy Spirit to work through you and the group discussion as you point to Jesus each week through God's Word.

Minimize Distractions

Create a comfortable environment. If group members are uncomfortable, they'll be distracted and therefore not engaged in the group experience. Plan ahead by considering these details:

Seating   **Temperature**   **Lighting**

Food & Drink   **Surrounding Noise**

General Cleanliness

At best, thoughtfulness and hospitality show guests and group members they're welcome and valued in whatever environment you choose to gather. At worst, people may never notice your effort, but they're also not distracted. Do everything in your ability to help people focus on what's most important: connecting with God, with the Bible, and with one another.

Include Others

Your goal is to foster a community in which people are welcome just as they are but encouraged to grow spiritually. Always be aware of opportunities to include any people who visit the group and to invite new people to join your group.

An inexpensive way to make first-time guests feel welcome or to invite people to get involved is to give them their own copies of this Bible-study book.

Encourage Discussion

A good small-group experience has the following characteristics.

EVERYONE PARTICIPATES. Encourage everyone to ask questions, share responses, or read aloud.

NO ONE DOMINATES—NOT EVEN THE LEADER. Be sure that your time speaking as a leader takes up less than half of your time together as a group. Politely guide discussion if anyone dominates.

NOBODY IS RUSHED THROUGH QUESTIONS. Don't feel that a moment of silence is a bad thing. People often need time to think about their responses to questions they've just heard or to gain courage to share what God is stirring in their hearts.

INPUT IS AFFIRMED AND FOLLOWED UP. Make sure you point out something true or helpful in a response. Don't just move on. Build community with follow-up questions, asking how other people have experienced similar things or how a truth has shaped their understanding of God and the Scripture you're studying. People are less likely to speak up if they fear that you don't actually want to hear their answers or that you're looking for only a certain answer.

GOD AND HIS WORD ARE CENTRAL. Opinions and experiences can be helpful, but God has given us the truth. Trust God's Word to be the authority and God's Spirit to work in people's lives. You can't change anyone but God can. Continually point people to the Word and to active steps of faith.

Keep Connecting

Think of ways to connect with group members during the week.

Participation during the group session is always improved when members spend time connecting with one another outside the group sessions. The more people are comfortable with and involved in one another's lives, the more they'll look forward to being together. When people move beyond being friendly to truly being friends who form a community, they come to each session eager to engage instead of merely attending.

Encourage group members with thoughts, commitments, or questions from the session by connecting through these communication channels:

Emails   **Texts**   **Social Media**

When possible, build deeper friendships by planning or spontaneously inviting group members to join you outside your regularly scheduled group time for activities like these:

Meals   **Fun Activities**

Projects around Your Home, Church, or Community

Week 1
RULER OF THE NATIONS

Start

Welcome to group session 1.

What sources have most shaped and informed your political views?

How helpful would it be to read a manual on assembling a dresser for baking a cake? Or consider how useful an owner's manual for a Honda might be for a Tesla. Manuals and instruction guides are good and helpful, but they are only good and helpful when used with the item they describe.

Many people look to the Bible as a kind of life manual when it comes to how to navigate family relationships, spiritual growth, or their relationship with God. We consult the Bible on church dynamics, personal choices, wisdom, and the spiritual life. Yet when it comes to politics, many people pick up Satan's manual, the world's manual, or even their favorite news channel's manual. None of these will prove to be to be as helpful as God's Word.

Why is it important to view the subject of politics from a biblical perspective?

What are some dangers in ignoring biblical principles related to politics and leaning on the world's political ideologies instead?

You simply cannot read the Bible and ignore the fact that God involves Himself with political affairs. As we read God's Word, we witness Him establishing nations, creating constitutions, dismantling nations or leadership. He makes laws and ordinances and dispenses wisdom to and through kings.

Unfortunately in our day, God and politics are disconnected from each other far too often. The failure to properly connect God's relationship to politics based on His Word has left individuals, leaders, and nations without of the knowledge needed to govern society as the Creator intended. As we start our study we'll learn how politics, governments, and our relationship to them is to run smoothly both for the benefit of the people and the glory of God.

Invite someone to pray, then watch the video teaching.

Watch

Use this page to take notes as you watch video session 1.

Discuss

Use the following questions to discuss the video teaching.

And on His robe and on His thigh He has a name written:
"KING OF KINGS, AND LORD OF LORDS."
REVELATION 19:16

This verse is the greatest political statement in all of Scripture. When Jesus returns to rule, He will be the visible ruler of the kings of the earth (Revelation 1:5). There will be no exit polls, no news cycles, no political posts, and certainly no election. He will establish His rule instantly.

In the meantime, Jesus rules from His heavenly position, where He remains sovereign over the kingdoms of this world (Colossians 1:16-17). Serving under His authority, kingdom-minded churches develop kingdom disciples who promote and advance God's kingdom agenda in the political realm. When this happens, we partner with Christ by manifesting His heavenly rule and authority in the world.

What are some practical ways kingdom disciples can help manifest Christ's authoritative rule on earth?

What are some ways believers in the past have mishandled their responsibility of stewarding politics leading to division rather than order?

The glory of God and the advancement of His kingdom is the central theme of Scripture. God governs His world through the principles rooted in His kingdom agenda, which is defined as *the visible manifestation of the comprehensive rule of God over every area of life.*

In the Bible, God's rule shows up through the establishment of four basic realms: the individual, the family, the church, and the society. These can also be defined as four forms of government functioning within God's kingdom agenda: self-government, family government, church government, and civil government. Each of these governments is defined biblically as a sphere of delegated authority.

Take a moment to talk through the four spheres of delegated authority and share how each passage relates to the specific category.

Self-Government: "For we must all appear before the judgment seat of Christ, so that each one may receive compensation for his deeds done through the body, in accordance with what he has done, whether good or bad." (2 Corinthians 5:10)

Family Government: "For I have chosen him, so that he may command his children and his household after him to keep the way of the Lord by doing righteousness and justice, so that the Lord may bring upon Abraham what He has spoken about him." (Genesis 18:19)

Church Government: In the same way He also took the cup after supper, saying, "This cup is the new covenant in My blood; do this, as often as you drink it, in remembrance of Me." (1 Corinthians 11:25)

Civil Government: Every person is to be subject to the governing authorities. For there is no authority except from God, and those which exist are established by God. (Romans 13:1; also see Romans 13:2-7)

God rules over all. While an institutional separation exists between church and state, neither the sacred and the secular nor God and politics should be separated. Our view of God will always be reflected in our politics, whether we want it to or not.

Describe why an understanding of God's rule over all informs God's rule over governing authorities. How does this show up in our engagement with political processes and ideals?

Let's kick-off our Bible study on Kingdom Politics in prayer.

Prayer

Lord, open our eyes and our hearts as we study this delicate yet all-important subject. Help us to learn to shape our views by Your Word to apply Your wisdom in every area of life, including our politics.

Hit the Streets
DESERT ISLAND GOVERNMENT

Imagine one day you find yourself fleeing from a shipwreck and being washed up on a solitary island in the vast ocean. The local people welcome you and appoint you their leader. Since you have no hope of rescue (and you are hungry and need a job), you decide to accept this assignment. Now you are faced with the question of how you should organize your newly formed government.

You skip the option of anarchy (the absence of government), after all you would be out of a job. You then consider other options such as: oligarchy (the rule by an elite few); monarchy (the rule by one supreme authority, perhaps a king or queen); ecclesiocracy (the rule by an institutional or state church); democracy (the rule of the citizenry); or perhaps, being originally from the United States, you might choose a constitutional republic (rule by the people through their chosen representatives who function under constitutional law).

Of course you would want to choose to govern according to the principles you knew from God's Word. As you consider your options, let these additional questions guide you to your decision.

Of the systems of government you know, what are the benefits and drawbacks of each?

In what ways do those governments align or conflict with godly principles?

Which most closely aligns with how you believe governments should function?

If you do ever find yourself on a solitary island, it is helpful to know God operates through decentralized, plural institutions, under His centralized leadership in order to produce self-government under Him. In other words, God has given men the ability and the authority to govern under His supreme authority.

It is crucial for us to understand that when each of the spheres of authority (individual, family, church, and civil government) operates as God designed them, they will flourish. This principle follows the command Moses told Israel to "keep the words of this covenant and do them, in order that you may be successful in everything that you do" (Deuteronomy 29:9). When people, families, churches, or a society operate with God as the ultimate source of authority, they put themselves in a position to be used by Him and experience His blessing.

Bible Study 1

WHEN JENGA GETS JUMBLED

Read Genesis 11:1-9 before completing the following study.

In Genesis 11:1-9, we read about a time in history when humanity first concocted a plan for world domination. They wanted to build a global society that would erase the Creator-creature distinction and dependence on God. They tried to centralize their power to "make a name" for themselves (Genesis 11:4).

In Scripture, a "name" symbolizes a definition of what something is. To name something was like establishing governance over it. When God told Adam to name all of the animals, God was setting Adam in a position of governance and responsibility over the animals he had named. That's one reason God changed people's names after they changed their relationship to Him in Scripture. The name change signified a new identity and allegiance.

The people who gathered together to "make a name" for themselves thought a one-world global community and government could eradicate the need for God because of their consolidated power. Yet, this was in direct disobedience to God's command in Genesis 9:1 to "be fruitful and multiply, and fill the earth." (See also Genesis 1:28.)

Why would God want to direct humanity to multiply and fill the earth instead of telling them to remain localized?

Name some purposes and strategies political leaders use today to "make a name" for themselves.

What at the dangers of making a name for ourselves as a societal goal?

What does Genesis 11:6 give as the reason for God's destruction of the tower and scattering of the people?

The people Babel marveled at their own creation as their tower became taller each day, and Scripture offers us an ironic comment in verse 5. Despite their craftsman-ship, they weren't so crafty that they achieved their goal of reaching the apex of heaven. God still had to come "down to see the city and the tower which the men had built" (Genesis 11:5).

It did not matter how proficient the people had become at building the tower or how much their technical expertise had developed. The people gathered together to define themselves and worship their own cleverness, and despite their best efforts, God still had to "come down" to see it. Men will never equal God.

What was the result of mankind's attempt at ultimate control?

What does this teach us about human limitations in ruling?

Read Isaiah 46:1-10. What does this passage teach about humanity's attempt to create "gods" or "power structures" on earth?

God is the sole power in the universe, and He does not allow any other claimants to the throne. God designed the governments of mankind to be decentralized (underneath His sole authority) and to operate through multiple human authori-ties that function with checks and balances.

What are some examples of decentralized governing authorities that operate with checks and balances?

The problem for power-hungry humans is that regardless of what we think, say, or try to create, we still depend on a Creator. Everything and everyone ultimately depends on God. He is the Creator and Sustainer of all life. As the builders in Babel discovered, the most people can do apart from God is rearrange what He has already made.

God operates as the sole Sovereign over His kingdom. All other authority is delegated and dispersed across multiple spheres of responsibility. Romans 13:1 supports this principle by encouraging believers to "subject to the governing authorities. For there is no authority except from God, and those which exist are established by God." Notice that *authorities* in this verse is plural. All "authorities" are established by God and are ultimately responsible to Him. These "pluralized" governments align with the four realms of self-government—family, church, and civil governments.

Why is shared and plural authority actually good for human flourishing?

The civil government is delegated the authority to promote and maintain justice, protect freedom, and defend its citizens. Because it functions under God as one of three institutions (alongside the family and the church), its role is designed to be limited. So, it functions best when the family and the church are taking up their own roles to equip individuals for better self-government.

What are some results that you have observed of the civil government stepping outside of its God-ordained role and taking up some of the responsibilities of the family and the church?

Note that the imperial power of Rome was the context of the civil government for many of the biblical references given about civil government (Romans 13:1; 1 Peter 2:13-15). In fact, the emperor was likely Nero who was remembered as one of the most oppressive rulers in history and was vilified for his persecution of the early Christians in Rome.

Paul and Peter still respected oppressive governments.
What does this teach us about our relationship to civil government?

What are some ways they resisted that government to follow Jesus?

How does trusting God as the Ruler of the nations and Jesus Christ as King of kings and Lord of lords shape your interactions with lesser authorities?

Closing

As we come to a close on today's personal reflection, take a moment to pray. Spend some time in prayer, asking God to align your heart and spirit with Him so that you can fully grasp His perspective on politics, civil government, and your relationship to it. You might also want to pray for your eyes of your heart to be opened to identify any spiritual warfare that takes place is today's political landscape. Ask God for discernment to recognize truth from falsehood. In doing so, you set yourself up to be a kingdom representative of His values relating to society.

Bible Study 2

AUTHORITY UNDER THE RULER OF NATIONS

We'll discuss the role of civil government more fully in the next session, but from God's perspective all government is rooted in levels of responsibility. All of His spheres of government—individual, family, church, and civil—rest on this reality. When functioning properly, each individual area of government produces accountability, responsibility, and productivity, starting in the individual sphere and working its way to the civil

For example, an individual who takes responsibility for self-government will strengthen the family government. A strong family government will contribute to healthy church governance. A healthy church impacts the wider realm of civil society.

Working backward, the civil government should promote justice so that the church, family, and individual can have the freedom to properly exercise their respective jurisdictions under God's authority.

How can a healthy family government impact the wider spheres of the church and civil government?

Read Matthew 5:13-16.

> *"You are the salt of the earth; but if the salt has become tasteless, how can it be made salty again? It is no longer good for anything, except to be thrown out and trampled underfoot by people. You are the light of the world. A city set on a hill cannot be hidden; nor do people light a lamp and put it under a basket, but on the lampstand, and it gives light to all who are in the house. Your light must shine before people in such a way that they may see your good works, and glorify your Father who is in heaven."*
> MATTHEW 5:13-16

How can the church take up this responsibility to influence the wider sphere of civil society as the "salt of the earth" and the "light of the world"?

How has the church inadvertently caused harm in the wider civil society by failing to be the "salt of the earth" and the "light of the world"?

The issues we face should lead us to the conclusion that we can't fix our problems alone. We can make all the mandates, take all the precautions, pass all the economic stimulus packages, and host international summits that we want, but if a spiritual root is erupting in rotten fruit, only God can solve the issues at hand. God will not allow any nation to solve its problems through political alliances alone. We desperately need to bring our faith into the civil and political arenas where God has placed us.

We have a decision to make: We can continue rebelling against God's rule, or we can challenge ourselves and our political leaders to return to God willingly and bring healing to our land. God's ultimate goal is for an international theocracy under the lordship of Jesus Christ (Psalm 2:1-12; 1 Corinthians 15:24-25). But until that day, God will still accomplish His goal for His creation on earth—whether we return to Him willingly or whether, like Babel, God has to come down and intervene for us to get right with Him.

What are some helpful and practical ways Christians can challenge political leaders to return to godly principles?

Name one thing you will commit to do to help the process of returning politics to its rightful place under God's rules.

Returning to God is the only way for us to experience redemption as a country and peace in our land. He is not far each of us, but we must recognize His sovereign rule (Acts 17:27). God wants the politics of our land, and how we discuss them, to reflect kingdom virtues—the set of values described in His Word. This happens when His followers prioritize pursuing a relationship with Him, which includes submitting to His ultimate rule. God has been and always will be the Ruler of the nations, and He wants all nations, languages, and people groups to praise Him (Psalm 2:10-12).

Read Revelation 7:9:

> *"After these things I looked, and behold, a great multitude which no one could count, from every nation and all the tribes, peoples, and languages, standing before the throne and before the Lamb, clothed in white robes, and palm branches were in their hands."*
>
> REVELATION 7:9

What does this passage reveal about where the whole world is headed?

How should this reality influence our present day relationship to civil politics and governance?

Scripture is clear that God is the sovereign ruler over His creation (Psalm 96:10). Sovereignty is the theological word that describes God's absolute right to govern the world He created according to His good pleasure. God's sovereignty is a crucial doctrine to grab hold of as we go through this study on kingdom politics because it describes what it means for God to be the ruler of the nations. It is to be kept in the forefront of our thoughts because it is the basis for God's authority. This doctrine makes it clear that God both rules and overrules.

Read the following passages on God's sovereignty and His rule over nations. Reflect on them by rephrasing them or responding to them in your own words:

> *"I know that You can do all things,*
> *And that no plan is impossible for You."*
>
> JOB 42:2

> *Whatever the Lord pleases, He does, in heaven and on earth, in the seas and in all the ocean depths.*
>
> PSALM 135:6

*It is He who changes the times and the periods; He removes
kings and appoints kings; He gives wisdom to wise men,
and knowledge to people of understanding.*
DANIEL 2:21

Do not move the ancient boundary which your fathers have set.
PROVERBS 22:28

*"Even from eternity I am He, and there is no one who can
rescue from My hand; I act, and who can reverse it?"*
ISAIAH 43:13

**What do these verses teach us about God's rule over the nations? Why is
this important for us to keep God's sovereignty over the nations in mind
throughout this study?**

Acknowledging God's sovereignty allows us to see lesser authorities from the
proper perspective. Because God is the ruler of the nations, nations function
best when they align themselves under His rule. When people and nations return
to God relationally under His kingdom rule, He can bring order and peace to a
chaotic environment (2 Chronicles 15:4,15).

Closing

Pray right now and ask God to guide us as a body of believers
to rally around His kingdom purposes for our nation. May He
deliver healing in our land, and may He use us to help bring
this about. Praise God for the times He has worked in history
and how we expect Him to work for His glory in our nation.

Week 2
THE PURPOSE
OF GOVERNMENT

Start

Welcome to group session 2.

Last session we discussed how God is the Ruler of the nations and began thinking about how our belief in God relates to our views of government.

What would you say are the main purposes of government?

In what ways have you benefited from the government?

Can you share one way you feel the government could improve to benefit the greater good of more people?

In the Bible, economics and charity resided in the family. God designed the family, not the church, to be first line of defense for material needs (1 Timothy 5:4-8). You shouldn't skip the family and go to the church. You would certainly not skip over both the family and the church and go straight to the federal government. That's not the way these spheres are designed to function.

This happens because many people have a dysfunctional understanding of government responsibility. The biblical role of civil government is *to maintain a safe, just, righteous, and compassionately responsible environment for freedom to flourish.*

People define freedom in many ways, so for the purposes of our time studying this subject together, freedom can be defined as *the release from illegitimate bondage so that you can choose to exercise responsibility in maximizing all that you were created to be.*

A civil government, operating under God's rule, primarily exist to protect citizens from enemies within (public safety) and enemies without (national defense) while establishing righteous laws in accordance with God's standard so that people can be unencumbered in their desire, determination, and ability to pursue their God-given potential.

Watch

Use this page to take notes as you watch video session 2.

Discuss

Use the following questions to discuss the video teaching.

Read Dr. Evans's definition of the role of government together:

The biblical role of civil government as established by the Creator of government, God Himself, is to maintain a safe, just, righteous and compassionately responsible environment for freedom to flourish.

What ideals are included in this definition? Where do you find support for those ideals in Scripture?

Read Romans 13:1-7 together.

Where do you find alignment between the scriptural foundation for government and Dr. Evans's definition?

Today people want God's name but not God's government. We place His name on our currency and in our pledge. We evoke His name at political rallies to gain points, but we're less interested in His view of government. We want what works best for us rather than what God has deemed best in His Word. Part of the reason we struggle and fight among ourselves today is that we have relegated God to the sidelines of our political discussions.

What are some ways we've removed God's perspective from governement? Be careful to apply this to yourself and not make this about other people.

In the video teaching, Dr. Evans compared the way we think of God in governement as the way people think about the King of England. Discuss this illustration together.

Charles III of England appears on currency. Everywhere he goes there is celebration and regalia. You know he's home because the flag outside of his house tells you so. No other human being enjoys such pomp and circumstance. But his authority is limited. He makes no law. He has no real say. His authority is in name only. If we aren't careful, we approach God the same way.

What steps can we take to make God the center of all that we do, including how we approach government?

What are some ways we can hold leaders accountable to the standards we find in Romans 13? Give concrete examples.

The closer a government is to God, the more ordered the society will be. The further the government is from God, the more chaotic the society will become. What kind of society do we want? We have the ability to seek God's best for our government and our society by following God's precepts and praying and advocating for others to do the same.

Read Matthew 22:15-22.

What should we render to Caesar (our government)?

What should we render to God?

Jesus used a coin bearing a government leader's image to teach His disciples a lesson. The tax was justly owed to Caesar as it bears His image, but His disciples—both then and today—bear God's image. We belong to Him, and everything that we do and all that we are is owed to Him. Our ultimate allegiance is to Him and His commands. As we interact with our government, we should remember that and continually call our rulers to meet the ultimate Ruler's standard.

Let's close our session this week in prayer.

Prayer

Father God, You have established government to protect the good and mitigate evil. You have ordered all things according to Your wisdom and will. Help us to place you at the center of our lives. Lead us to call our leaders to follow Your standard so that we can influence society for good.

Hit the Streets
BLESSING IN THE RAIN

Imagine that you are about to head out to an evening concert with family or friends. You look outside the window and see that it is raining. You quickly check your weather app to get an idea of when the rain will stop. The weather app tells you that rather than stopping, the rain is actually going to fall harder over the next hour.

List three things you grab to bring with you.

A covenant is like an umbrella. An umbrella doesn't stop it from raining—an umbrella just stops the rain from reaching you. The umbrella covers you so you don't have to experience the effects of the rain. Similarly, God covers those who are covenantally-aligned under Him. He doesn't stop the storms or calm all chaos, but He provides covering in it. This is why Christians must ascribe ourselves first to the superintending governance of God, not to a political party.

To the degree that we operate under this covenantal umbrella through aligning our actions and policies under God we will experience the goodness of God in our land. In this manner, we will also encourage goodness and righteousness in those who rule our land. Here are three ways you can operate under God's covenantal umbrella with regard to politics:

1. Invite open discussions on God's values and principles related to politics in conversations in your community and church as well as in letters or emails to your local and national political representatives. But as you do this, remember the next way.

2. Speak to others with a tone of kindness and love. The greatest commandment God gives is to love Him, followed by the second commandment to love others. When Christians join in on hateful, dishonoring speech, memes, and accusations, they have moved out from under God's best umbrella (Matthew 22:36-40; Ephesians 4:15).
3. Relinquish your need to always have others see you as being right or to have the last say. Surrendering to God by living with peace and His glory as your goals will diffuse much of the division Satan capitalizes on, especially during political seasons. It also leaves room for the Spirit to work in the other people's lives, hearts, and minds.

If you will commit to do these three things regularly and with a sincere heart, you can experience more of God's covenantal covering with regard to politics. Doing these things may not be easy, but you will find help to do them when you look to the Holy Spirit and walk according to the power He gives you.

How will you engage political discussion differently this week based on your relationship with God?

Bible Study 1

GOVERNMENT REFLECTS GOD

When God established the nation Israel, He gave them the law which is encapsulated in Ten Commandments. In addition to the Ten Commandments, God also gave them 613 statutes and ordinances. These statutes and ordinances provided the framework for which the application of the Ten Commandments would be carried out in culture. Together these laws describe God's character and protect the well-being of society.

Read Exodus 20:1-17. What blessings would come to Israel for obeying these? What effects might they bring by disobeying them?

Choose two of the Ten Commandments and write down the blessing that comes from embracing them and the effect that comes from disregarding them.

Commandment 1:

Blessing:

Effect:

Commandment 2:

Blessing :

Effect:

Remember, biblical role of civil government is *to maintain a safe, just, righteous and compassionately responsible environment for freedom to flourish.* Embracing God's standard always invites blessing and flourishing. Disregarding it always leads to sin and struggle. If Adam obeyed God's command he could experience the full blessing of eating from all the trees, but when he broke the command (with Eve) he was thrown out of the garden (Genesis 2:15-17). This was no less true for the people of Israel in their covenant with God. Joshua, the leader of Israel after Moses, was commanded to "be careful to do according to all the Law which Moses My servant commanded you; do not turn from it to the right or to the left, so that you may achieve success wherever you go" (Joshua 1:7).

What would be the promised "effect" for Joshua if he chose to obey God's commands and align himself underneath God's covenantal rule?

What would change about our nation and its government if people embraced God's standards as a covenantal way of life?

Though God's standard was first given to His people from Adam to Noah to Abraham and then to Israel in the Ten Commandments, His standard applies to all nations. As we saw, God is the ultimate Ruler of all nations. If you want to see your nation healed and helped, you need to re-insert God's person and perspective into politics wherever and however you can. If you are tired of witnessing decay in your nation, then you need to emphasize God's perspective in political discussions and actions. God initiated government, and it can be a mechanism for society to experience God's blessing.

Do you view government as a way to bring God's blessing or do you cynically disregard God's ability to bring blessing through righteous government? Explain.

List three ways you can pray for politicians, our elections, and the overall collective conversation regarding politics in order for it to improve.

Read Romans 13:1-4.

Are there exceptions to the command to "subject to the governing authorities" (v. 1)? Why or why not?

Are there occasions that warrant rebelling against a governing authority? Explain.

Romans 13:4 says a ruler is "God's minister." The word here is the same as the word for "deacon." How can government authorities act as ministers of God?

What are some ways you see government leaders ministering on God's behalf?

According to the book of Romans, all civil government is established by God and set in place to restrain and punish evil and to reward and promote good. This does not legitimize everything the government may do (because "a legitimate office can act in illegitimate ways"), but it does mean government is in place because God has willed it. So, we have a responsibility to submit to it as an authority under God.

What are some ways you can remind and encourage civil servants to embrace the role God has called them to?

What are some ways you as an individual follower of Christ can contribute to your nation being the kind of safe, just, righteous, and compassionately responsible environment God wants it to be?

God's people have been drawn into a covenant with Him by grace through faith in Jesus Christ. One of the blessings of that covenant is that we can contribute to the kind of environment God intends for our government to create. As we pursue God individually and together with our families and our churches, God's influence in and through us will reach out into civil society and reshape it according to His standards.

This is a gift and responsibility for all kingdom citizens. We all have a part to play, and as we play our part, our civil government will flourish. When that happens, we will experience the blessing God intends for us and avoid the sin and struggle that comes from living outside of God's covenant with us.

Closing

As we close this session, spend some time praying about how you can influence our society for good. Do a personal assessment of your engagement in the political realm by action or word. Make it a point of personal focus to grow in positive influence related to the area of kingdom politics, and seek the Spirit's leading as you do.

Bible Study 2
CHECKS AND BALANCES

The further you remove God's person and His policies from politics, the further you remove the nation from a position of blessing, power and covering. You leave the nation exposed to all manner of attack, vulnerabilities, destruction, and infiltration. One natural way a government is to reflect God and bring about just governance is through checks and balances.

The idea of checks and balances reflects an idea that we find throughout the Bible—unity in diversity. We see this in God Himself (three distinct Persons in one God), in godly marriage (two complimentary yet distinct genders in one union), and in the church (one body with a variety of gifts).

What are some of the basic benefits of a government founded on "checks and balances" allowing both unity and diversity?

What can happen to a nation when there are no working "checks and balances"?

How do checks and balances allow godly citizens to play a pivotal role in their own governance?

If God has been removed from a government's functions, the character of its leaders, and the values of its citizens, those prayers will often go unanswered. Leaving God out of the equation of a nation also removes God's intervention and blessing on the nation. God's principles are never to be separated from the over-arching governance of a land rooted in God's principles. We can see this in two distinctives that exists in all covenants: hierarchy and oaths.

HIERARCHY: Each of God's covenants are administered through a chain of command that functions under His ultimate authority. In 1 Corinthians 11:3 Paul stated, "I want you to know that the head of every man is Christ, the head of woman is man, and the head of Christ is God." This means everyone in God's kingdom functions under authority, under a "head." Even though Jesus is the eternal Son who is co-equal with God the Father, in His earthly ministry, Jesus submitted to the Father's will. God's statutes and covenants assume a hierarchy.

How does this principle relate to a system of checks and balances?

What are some ways we can show respect for God's chain of command?

How does this principle extend to our homes, workplaces, churches, and society?

OATHS: Each of God's covenants contained an oath or a pledge that the covenant partner must make. This oath or pledge outlined the blessings for obedience and the curses for disobedience that were binding for the covenant partner. The clearest example of this is in Deuteronomy 27–30, where Moses read to Israel the list of blessings and curses attached to God's covenant with His people. Moses closed out the list with a final warning to the people saying, "I have placed before you life and death, the blessing and the curse" (Deuteronomy 30:19).

What are some modern day examples of oaths that bind the oath-taker to specific rules, stipulations, and guidelines?

How does our oath to be kingdom citizens manifest itself in our political engagement?

A nation is blessed when it recognizes God is over it (Psalm 33:12). Without God's rule and perspective to guide and to govern, a nation will devolve into chaos and anarchy. It will become an oppressive society because it adheres to a "freedom" that has no standards. Simply stated, the closer a nation is to God's person and principles, the more ordered that society will be. The further that nation is from God and His principles, the more chaotic and oppressive that society will become.

God has designed each of the four spheres of government (personal, family, church, and society) within the kingdom agenda to operate by balancing love and discipline within their assigned jurisdictions. For example, the civil government is to reward good and discipline those who break the laws (Romans 13:3). Also, within the family government, parents are to love their children and to "bring them up in the discipline and instruction of the Lord" (Ephesians 6:4).

What examples can you think of within civil government where the balance is tipped and we focus too heavily on love?

What examples can you think of within civil government where the balance is tipped and we focus too heavily on discipline?

Why is it important for each of these areas to have consequences for disobedience?

How does this balance of love and discipline help us maintain better self-governance?

What might it look like to exercise discipline in the sphere of self-government?

Those who govern in politics are to reflect God's values in reinforcing good behavior and policing against evil. Roman soldiers were considered the policemen of their day. As part of their uniform, they would carried a sword. The sword was for two things: intimidation and judgment. The goal in intimidation was to limit potential bad behavior from taking place before it even got started. But the second reason the Roman soldiers carried the sword was for judgment, which included capital punishment, whether for evil acts committed by the citizenry or by the leaders. The sword meant evil would not go ignored.

This was their way of maintaining a safe and just environment for the people. Freedom cannot flourish in any nation apart from safety. Freedom cannot flourish in any nation apart from justice and righteousness. Freedom flourishes when governments rule according to God's standards. And when they do not, it is our role as believers in the body of Christ to pray for them. In fact, we are to pray for politicians and civil servants as a regular part of our prayer life (1 Timothy 2:2). It is also our responsibility to respectfully challenge them when they clearly deviate from God's standards (1 Samuel 15:10-23; Matthew 14:1-4).

Closing

As we close out this week's session, spend some time praying for politicians and civil servants according to God's values and principles. Ask the Holy Spirit to guide you in your prayers so that you will live as an effective spiritual warrior with regard to kingdom politics.

6 *What*... we have...
We have...

7 Our fathers understood not thy
wonders in... thy
multitude...
They remembered not the multitude of thy...
8 But were rebellious at the sea,
even at the Red Sea.
Nevertheless he saved them
for his name's sake,
That he might make his mighty
power to be known.
9 He rebuked the Red Sea also,
and it was dried up:

26 There... all...
thou...
therein.
27 These wait all...
That thou mayest...
their food in due season.
28 That thou givest unto them they
gather;
Thou openest thine hand, they
are satisfied with good.
29 Thou hidest thy face, they are
troubled;

1 Heb. *To make his face to shine with oil*
2 Or. *creatures*   3 Or. *with him* See Job 41.5

He shorte...

1 Or. *is stretched out*   2 Or...
3 Heb. *Jah*   4 Heb. *the children*
5 Another reading is, *afflicted me with* ...
strength

7 He is...
His judgments...
earth.
8 He hath...
nant for ever...

roaring   3 Heb. *Jah*   3 Or. *instructeth*

Thou... with...
rulest...
The heavens are...
earth also is thine:
the world and the fulness
thereof, thou hast founded
them.

2 Or. *sons* of God

107 Oh give than...
For his lovingkin...
for ever.
2 Let the redeem...
say so;

Week 3
FOUNDATIONS OF KINGDOM GOVERNMENT

Start

Welcome to group session 3.

Last week we studied the purpose of government, and this week we will study the foundational principles of government.

What was one significant truth you learned last week?

Imagine if you or a family member were sick and you went to the doctor to find out what was wrong. After the appointment, the doctor told you that if you took the medication he or she prescribed, you or your family member would get better. This would undoubtedly be a relief to hear. But what would happen if you went to the pharmacy with the right prescription only to have it filled with the wrong medication? The "written document" from the doctor may have been right but when it was enacted the wrong way in the fulfillment at the pharmacy, you or your family member would be messed up.

Similarly, in politics and the governance of a land, you can't have right written rules (righteousness) without the proper fulfillment of those rules (justice) if citizens are going to be well in the nation. Without righteousness and justice working together, freedom wanes and society becomes messed up.

How would you define the terms *freedom*, *righteousness*, and *justice*?

Understanding these three core concepts and how they relate helps us gain insight into the way God established government and politics to operate. The biblical role of government is *to maintain a safe, just, righteous and compassionately responsible environment for freedom to flourish.* Righteousness is *the standard of right and wrong that has been established by God.* Justice is the *impartial and equitable application of God's moral law in society.* Together, they produce freedom.

Invite someone to pray, then watch the video teaching.

Watch

Use this page to take notes as you watch video session 3.

Discuss

Use the following questions to discuss the video teaching.

When a young child decides to play dangerously near a cliff, a loving parent yells "Stop!" No one would fault parents for limiting their child's freedom to protect that child from harm. Some radicals may view the presence of a fence as a limitation of the child's freedom. But a good parent views the fence as a boundary that enhances the child's freedom to play without fear of injury.

Why is the presence of healthy boundaries not a limitation on freedom?

God is our perfect Father. He gives us freedom within boundaries, not to prevent us from exercising our freedom, but to help us use our freedom in a way that won't lead to harm. God has established government to create boundaries that enhance citizens' freedom and limit harm. Examining the biblical foundation for true freedom and its implications gives us wisdom on kingdom politics.

Read John 8:31-36. According to this passage, how should we define freedom?

Describe the kind of freedom we have in Jesus Christ? Share how you have benefited from this freedom?

America was founded on the principle of freedom—freedom of religion, freedom of speech, and the freedom to pursue one's dreams. Our founders were certain to include these all-important freedoms because they knew firsthand what their absence could lead to for the citizenry. But this freedom would be couched in personal responsibility and boundaries because without these, freedom can't exist. The absence of boundaries doesn't lead to true freedom; it leads to anarchy and chaos. God has established moral boundaries, not because He wants to ruin our fun but because He wants us to experience joy. When we're entangled in sin or trying to find satisfaction outside of a relationship with Christ, we don't have freedom. But when we live in fellowship with God and follow His guidelines for life, we can fully exercise our freedom. True freedom starts with submission to God and His Word.

Read Galatians 5:13. How does the freedom we have in Christ make us responsible to God and others?

Name a few examples of the kinds of responsibilities that come with freedom.

Freedom also includes responsibility. When we read Genesis 2:15, we see that God put Adam in the garden and gave him a job. God gave Adam the responsibility to tend to the plants and trees and to protect the garden from the influence of Satan. In the pre-fall part of Adam's life, he had more freedom than we have ever known. Yet along with freedom, God gave Adam a task. In Christ, we have true freedom, but that freedom comes with the responsibility to love God and serve others.

Why do we tend to view boundaries and responsibilities as a barrier to freedom instead of necessary to it?

On the whole, does your life reflect freedom and joy that come from Christ or the bondage and chaos that result from ignoring Him? Explain.

The more a nation's laws reflect God's standards, and the more a government doesn't overstep its boundaries and misuse its power, the more the society will encourage individual freedom. As Christ followers, we must use our freedom to take personal responsibility for our actions, including supporting candidates and policies that reflect God's kingdom agenda.

Let's close our session this week in prayer.

Prayer

Lord, help me live responsibly in a way that upholds the freedoms of others while also experiencing the benefits of Your blessings. Show me how to appreciate healthy boundaries so I can flourish as I seek to serve You.

Hit the Streets

FREEDOM FOUNDED IN TRUTH

The foundation of freedom is both knowing and living in accordance with truth. As John 8:32 says, "the truth will set you free." But what is truth? The truth that we as individuals and our society as a whole must live by is the truth of the gospel—that Jesus is the Son of God who lived a perfect life, died on the cross to pay for our sins, rose from the dead victorious over sin and death, and ascended to the right hand of the Father where He rules and reigns. True freedom starts with freedom from bondage to sin and the penalty of sin.

We can only take the first step toward freedom if we know the truth.

Unfortunately, sometimes feelings get in the way of knowing the truth. Our emotions are powerful but are not always accurate reflectors of truth. While emotions may indicate the changing state of our internal lives, God's Word is the unchanging barometer by which we can measure our emotions, thoughts, and decisions. Even facts may only give us a partial view of reality. But God's Word provides absolute truth amid unreliable facts and emotions.

Read 1 Samuel 15:1-9. What did God command King Saul to do? Did King Saul obey God?

Read 1 Samuel 15:10-16. What was King Saul's emotional state when Samuel came to him (v. 13)? Was Saul's emotional state an accurate barometer for whether or not he was obedient to God? Why or why not?

Think of a time when you elevated either your emotions or facts above God's truth. What happened?

Those working in the area of politics, and also politicians, often rely on emotions to gain power. Follow these three steps when seeking to discern between emotional rhetoric and truth (both internally and externally):

1. Identify the root of the event, action or topic apart from the memes, messaging and manipulations around it.
2. Ask God to reveal wisdom to you through His Word as you seek His insight on the truth on the topic, person, politician, or policy.
3. Seek to align your thoughts and your words (how you speak about it) on the subject under God's revealed truth in His Word.

If you will commit to doing these three things on a regular basis, you will begin to see your influence increase in kingdom politics.

In what situations are you most tempted to follow your emotions instead of the truth?

Which of the steps above would be most helpful to you in those moments? Why?

BIBLICAL JUSTICE

The prophet Habakkuk watched as the people of Judah—God's people—practiced injustice, oppressed the poor, and mocked God's covenant. Though Habakkuk called the people to repent and warned them that judgment was coming, they refused to listen. He said,

> *Therefore the Law is ignored,*
> *And justice is never upheld.*
> *For the wicked surround the righteous;*
> *Therefore justice comes out confused.*
> HABAKKUK 1:4

Habakkuk longed for God to discipline His people and rule over them with His perfect justice. Idolatry resided at the core of Judah's injustice. They worshiped false gods, who are really just demons in disguise (1 Corinthians 10:19-20), and these demons led God's people to pervert justice.

When Christ isn't on the throne of our hearts and our nation, it's no wonder that prejudice, greed, pride, and lawlessness flourish. If the church wants to influence our nation for the better, we have to model biblical justice. We must follow Jesus and share the uncompromising truth of salvation through Him alone, while also seeking to alleviate their afflictions.

As the perfect example of grace and truth, Jesus addressed people's spiritual and physical diseases. Just as Jesus imparted biblical justice to all who came into contact with Him, the church today must do the same, bringing God's kingdom agenda to earth.

Read Luke 4:14-30. According to this passage, how should we define biblical justice?

How should the church promote biblical justice in our society?

One of the arguments I often hear from those who disagree on the church's role in promoting biblical justice is that the church should be about the gospel. I agree—it should. But what we often miss is that the scope of the gospel includes carrying out biblical justice. So, how do justice and the gospel work together? To overemphasize one or the other could lead to error. Let's look at justice and the gospel holistically to see how the idea of justice plays out in Scripture.

THE CONTENT AND SCOPE OF THE GOSPEL

Read 1 Corinthians 15:1-4.

How would you articulate the content of the gospel in your own words?

To understand how the gospel achieves God's justice, we must differentiate the content and scope of the gospel. The content of the gospel is pretty clear—"Christ died for our sins according to the Scriptures, and that He was buried, and that He was raised on the third day according to the Scriptures" (1 Corinthians 15:3-4). Belief in the content of the gospel results in forgiveness and eternal life.

So, what's the scope of the gospel? The scope of the gospel includes God's power to save, His righteousness, as well as our justification, sanctification, and future glorification. The gospel's scope also includes our conduct, love for others who are not like us or who may be our enemies, and whether or not we live by God's standard of justice.

Read Habakkuk 2:4. Describe the connection between faith and righteousness in this verse. How does pride stifle our ability to live out the gospel?

What is the scope of the gospel in your life? How can you infuse God's justice into your relationships?

JESUS AND THE GOSPEL

Glance back at Luke 4:14-30.

When Jesus announced His public ministry He defined His purpose by quoting from Isaiah 61. Part of what identified Jesus as the Messiah was His manifestation of God's justice. Jesus shared the gospel with the poor, the captives, the blind, and the oppressed. He met their spiritual needs and their physical needs.

How would you compare the needs in Jesus's day to the needs in ours?

How are you meeting needs and seeking justice the way that Jesus did?

THE DAY OF ATONEMENT

Read Leviticus 25:9-10.

The year of the Lord's favor that Jesus talked about was known as the year of Jubilee. During this year, which occurred every fiftieth year, all debts were forgiven and all slaves were set free. The Day of Atonement—the one day each year during which the high priest slaughtered an animal to atone for the peoples' sins (Leviticus 16:29-34)—inaugurated the Jubilee. It's important to realize that forgiveness for sins (the content of the gospel) preceded the Jubilee when people received economic, social, and political freedom (the scope of the gospel).

Read Leviticus 25. What do you observe about God in this chapter? How does prove His care for His land, the poor, foreigners, and slaves?

How should God's care be matched by Christian citizens participating in civil government?

CHRIST AS KING

The Roman government oppressed Jews in Jesus's day. The Jews wanted so badly to be freed from Roman tyranny that they didn't see the true freedom Jesus offered. Part of the reason they crucified Him was because He taught them to submit to political authorities, love their enemies, and wait for a future kingdom. Like many people today, they wanted all the benefits of God's justice now without submitting to His sovereignty and believing in His gospel. Instead, we should trust in Christ's death and resurrection, and then share the gospel with others, meeting their spiritual, emotional, and physical needs. This order reflects God's kingdom agenda on earth. Are you willing to ask God to increase your ability to promote biblical justice?

How can we carry out both the spiritual and physical aspects of the gospel in our lives?

On a scale of 0-10 (with 10 being the highest), how would you rate the body of Christ in America when it comes to living out and speaking up for biblical justice in society?

0   1   2   3   4   5   6   7   8   9   10

On a scale of 0-10 (with 10 being the hightest), how would you rate yourself in the same area?

0   1   2   3   4   5   6   7   8   9   10

Closing

Close out today's study by spending time in prayer, asking the Holy Spirit to pour out His blessing and power on our nation and to enable believers to live with great courage. Ask for a greater level of biblical justice and righteousness to be made evident in our land.

Bible Study 2
FREEDOM AND JUSTICE

When God established the entity known as government, He created it with the idea of limited regulations. We witness this first and foremost in the governance set forth in the garden for Adam and Eve. Adam and Eve were free to eat from any of the trees they wanted, except for one. This was our first exposure of limited governance.

What are some benefits of limited government?

What are some cautions of limited government?

We also witness limited government when we look at how God created. Israel was established in the format for the way a society is supposed to run and civil government is supposed to function. When we think in terms of Israel as a nation and its government, most of us tend to reflect on the Ten Commandments, as we should. These ten commandments established the non-negotiable boundaries for how a civil society should run. They were specific in nature, but they were also limited in scope. There were just these ten things to live by in order to have a free society where everyone could fully maximize his or her potential.

What's more, when God introduced the Ten Commandments, He did so with a statement that many people miss. He provides the context for the commandments in His opening line, which is, "I am the LORD your God, who brought you out of the land of Egypt, out of the house of slavery" (Exodus 20:2). In this revealing opening statement, God reminded the people of Israel that He is the One who gave them their freedom in the first place. He is the One who set them free from the land of Egypt and their house of slavery. Since He provided the freedom, He had the right to set the boundaries in which they were to function. Those boundaries were designed to create opportunity for citizens to take full advantage of freedom.

What can happen when boundaries are set up apart from loving-kindness and righteousness?

Based on His own examples, God defines the healthy running of a civil government as one that maximizes freedom and offers limited regulations but also attaches significant consequences when those regulations are broken. The closer a government is to God's government, the more ordered society will be. The further a government is from God's prescribed method of ruling according to both righteousness and justice, the more chaotic the culture will become.

Civil government is to allow maximum freedom of the good things God has provided for people to have the opportunity and option to exercise personal responsibility. It does this through the enactment of regulations coupled with consequences. The government will succeed to the degree that they establish and operate by righteousness and justice as God defines them. The Bible is clear that God's throne (kingdom) runs this way. The casual reading of Scripture clearly demonstrates how often these two concepts are intimately connected. (For example, see Deuteronomy 32:4; Job 37:23; Psalm 33:5; 97:2; 99:4; Isaiah 51:5; 56:1; 28:17; 32:16; 33:5; 56:1; Amos 5:24; and Romans 3:26.)

We can't expect secular political institutions and unbelievers to live by God's standards of biblical justice. The church must demonstrate God's justice in the way they interact within the church and with their communities. Here are three ways we can promote these standards within our culture:

PERSONAL LIFE

Christians should make living by Micah 6:8 a priority.
When we practice justice, kindness, and humility, others will notice.

Read Micah 6:8. If you were to take God's mandate seriously, how would that affect your family, school, employer, church, and friends?

Think of one person in your life who needs justice, one who needs kindness, and one who could benefit from your humility. How might you display Micah 6:8 to these people this week?

FAMILY LIFE

Family is the best place to teach and practice biblical justice. As Christians, let's raise the next generation of adults who will practice personal responsibility, live with kindness and humility, and empower others to do the same.

Read Genesis 18:19. What responsibility do Christian parent bear to teach their children to obey the Lord and seeking righteousness and justice?

If you have children, how can you teach them about God's justice and help them live by Micah 6:8?

CHURCH LIFE

Read James 2:1-9.

The church should be the last place on earth where we find prejudice, cliques, and favoritism. Unfortunately, many churches disintegrate because of these injustices. Since all people have been created in God's image and have equal worth in His eyes, the body of Christ should be a place of mutual encouragement and equality.

Read Ephesians 4:1-6. How can memorizing these verses help us stay away from favoritism, cliques, and prejudices?

Have you ever been excluded from a clique? How did that make you feel?

Christians don't spread God's justice by secluding themselves, locking the doors of the church, and hiding out inside. Christians must infiltrate every area of our secular society armed with biblical justice.

Psalm 72:1-2 says, "Give the king Your judgments, O God, And Your righteousness to the king's son. May he judge Your people with righteousness and Your afflicted with justice." This passage reminds us that God intends human governments to be instruments of His justice.

Believers should get involved in the law-making process by running for office, contacting their representatives, and exercising their right to vote. God also calls His people into various vocations to carry out His justice. If you're a doctor, a lawyer, a teacher, a secretary, a pastor, or a stay at home mom, the Lord wants you to be an instrument of biblical justice in your specific area of influence.

How is God asking you to pursue justice and righteousness in the spheres where you have influence?

What are some ways individuals, families, and churches pursuing justice and righteousness today can expand outward to make a more just and righteous culture?

Closing

Close by asking God to reveal which of the three areas listed above you need to focus on the most for personal growth. Where can you improve in your walk with God so that others will benefit from your spiritual maturity and wisdom? Take a moment to pray and ask the Holy Spirit to honor your heart's desire with His help, teaching, and guidance.

Week 4
THE VALUES OF THE KINGDOM

Start

Welcome to group session 4.

Last week we looked at foundational value for government—freedom, righteousness, and justice. This week we will see how those values translate into policies.

Describe your understanding of what it means to protect the right to life.

What are some ways people seek to protect life in the womb but disregard the rights people need "to the tomb" once born?

Today we live on a battlefield where various kingdoms are vying for influence. The competing kingdoms of entertainment, sports, social media, and, of course, politics are all seeking to capture one strategic asset—the family. Their aim is to supersede and redefine the family's influence in the home. The family is the first institution established by God that would serve as the foundation for the wellbeing of society and civilization. Whoever owns the family owns the future.

When the family structure breaks down, all manner of calamity and chaos enter into society. Crime, poverty, abuse, gender confusion, and a myriad of other issues arises.

It is the role of civil government to promote and protect the family as God created it to be as well as the right to life for all people. Psalm 89:14 tells us that God is a God of both righteousness and justice. Yet, it often seems, the body of Christ is split down the middle with some on one side calling for righteousness in the protection of life in the womb but some on the other side calling for justice in the protection of life and dignity outside of the womb—you have a house divided. Strengthening the family involves supporting both.

We must call for the protection of life in the womb and to the tomb. We must not subscribe to a term-life agenda. Believers are to pursue a whole-life agenda because that is what God instructs us in His Word. He calls for a kingdom agenda for all of life. Satan seeks to destroy family's by any means possible. We must stand up for all life.

Invite someone to pray, then watch the video teaching.

Watch

Use this page to take notes as you watch video session 4.

Discuss

Use the following questions to discuss the video teaching.

How do you define the word *family*?

In a culture where every role and relationship within the family—from the husband-wife relationship to the parent-child relationship—is in the process of redefinition, it can be difficult to know for sure what "family" should look like. The family, and the dignity of life itself, go hand in hand. Where the family unit breaks down, the value and dignity of life also erodes. Where the family unit is strong, life is valued, cherished, and preserved. Kingdom politics aims to protect the family unit, and as a result, the right of life for all.

Why should we see the family as a foundational pillar in society?

In what way does a strong family unit also protect the right to life for the vulnerable in the womb?

How has the destruction of the family unit lowered the dignity and value for life itself?

One thing American Christians and non-Christians can agree on—the family unit is falling apart. And as a result, our society is crumbling. While there are many efforts to fix the cracks, they are just the symptoms of a shifting family foundation. The breakdown of the family is the single most basic reason for the disintegration of our society and culture. If we don't solidify the foundation of the family, we will forever be doing social patchwork. When God created the world and the first society, He started by establishing the family with a specific purpose in mind.

Read Genesis 18:18-19 and Proverbs 22:6. What are some practical ways for parents to teach their kids "the way of the LORD" (v. 19)?

Can you share a Bible verse that helps you or that you have heard helps others who are struggling to understand the value of life, the value of family, or both?

God has used the institution of family to fulfill His purposes throughout history. From the flood to the creation of the people of Israel, God used families to accomplish His will. God so values the family that He called the Israelites His bride and His children. He called the church the "household of the faith" and referred to Christians as brothers and sisters in Christ (Galatians 6:10). When God the Father sent His Son to redeem the world, He placed Jesus into a family to learn, grow, and love with a father, mother, siblings, and extended family. God prepared Jesus to lay down His life for all people in the context of family. And now, through redemption in Jesus Christ, families can find restoration when the members who make up the family choose to align themselves under God and His kingdom rule.

How do the terms the Bible uses help us understand the importance of family?

List some families in the biblical narrative God used to expand His kingdom.

God has woven the thread of family and its role in expanding His kingdom throughout Scripture. Only as we maintain the foundation of the family can we see the expansion of God's kingdom in the world as it was designed to be including acting as a vehicle for restoration and for blessing.

How can kingdom politics support the concept of family?

How can politics by the world's agenda tear down the family?

Let's close our session this week in prayer.

Prayer

Lord, help us understand Your kingdom values, especially those affected deeply by politics, laws, regulations, and cultural influences. Help us gain insight into why Your values are what they are, and how we can uphold them through all means, even through the strategic use and influence on politics.

Hit the Streets
A VOICE FOR TRUTH

One of the reasons so few people find the courage to stand up for values like the right to life or issues of biblical justice is due to the separatism and schisms that exist in the church. When a person feels alone in his or her beliefs, it can become harder to be a voice for truth.

While "freedom of religion" is a great thing, it has also led to freedom from religion as well as freedom of divergent religious beliefs, which causes different denominations to be offered on every corner. So many options of belief leads to moral relativism and a lack of commitment, which contributes to the secularization of society. While freedom of religion is good, we need to also seek to unify on shared values to impact our nation. Here are some things we can do. Consider how your group may take part:

Seek ways to collectively address shortages of food, housing, and other basic needs of underserved families in your community or of young mothers with unplanned pregnancies.

Equip and/or shape the mindset of church members with regard to a kingdom perspective as they engage with the culture.

Connect with local law enforcement to foster a stronger relationship and serve as a bridge between the police and the community.

Construct a network for business leaders who want to assist in creating employment opportunities for the disenfranchised.

Identify key service agencies in your community that you can collectively support to facilitate a beneficial kingdom impact.

Work with kids in the foster care system or support an organization that fights human trafficking.

Coordinate a collective voice in petitions, letter writing, phone calls,
and other ways to influence political leadership to bring about righteous
and just policy and legislative reforms.

Nationwide positive impact is never easy, but it is easier when like-minded individuals unite under an umbrella of shared kingdom values. When we do this, we can make a difference.

Which of these opportunities could you take advantage of?

What other ideas do you have to support the underserved and build up
individuals and families from a whole life (womb to tomb) perspective?

Spend some time praying that God would prepare you and your family
for whole life impact for the benefit of His kingdom.

Bible Study 1
FAMILY, CHURCH, COMMUNITY

On the sixth day of creation, God created human beings to reflect His triune image. The ultimate mission of families is to bear the image of the Father, Son, and Spirit through furthering God's kingdom and rule on this earth.

In the triune Godhead each person is fully unique yet together they comprise the unified Godhead. Similarly, in marriage, man and woman mirror God through their individual personalities and unified essence as one married couple.

Read Genesis 1:26-28. In what ways do you reflect God's image?

How does the family structure created by God mirror God's image and goodness?

All human beings and specifically all human faimlies are supposed to mirror God in the world. In this way, the family a kind of visible photograph of the invisible God.

Compare the quote above to what society says the goal of families should be and what God says.

What do we lose if we seek to define a family apart from God's character and design?

God created families is to fulfill His plan of implementing His dominion in history. By delegating control to us, God indirectly controls the affairs of the world through our rule on His behalf. He doesn't force us to rule but allows us to exercise dominion over His creation. Dominion simply means ruling on God's behalf according to His values.

Why is exercising our dominion on earth important?

How have we fallen short of managing our earthly responsibilities according to God's command?

Read Genesis 3:1-5. How did Eve faith to exercise dominion? What implications does this have in our understanding of why mankind often fails to exercise proper dominion over creation?

In what ways do you see Satan seeking to disrupt the political realm to get Christians out from under God's authority and to keep them from supporting His kingdom values?

God establishes the type of relationship He is to have with mankind by revealing His authority, and He has placed the family unit under His divine authority. Throughout Genesis 2, we read the phrase, "The LORD God." This phrase explains God's authoritative nature and absolute control over all creation, including the family. The word LORD, when written in all capital letters, refers to God's name, which is Yahweh. The translation of Yahweh is "master, and absolute ruler."

Kingdom Politics

Why is God's authority important to our understanding of the family structure related to politics?

Why is it important to understand family, not politics is the primary building block of society? What happens when we confuse the two?

Strong families sustain strong churches, which then enables the church to function according to God's prescribed plans. But when Satan is allowed to dismantle the family unit, then churches also suffer. This lack of strength in the churches opens the door for governments to begin functioning in roles of family with regard to provision, values training, and more.

Read Deuteronomy 8:11-18. According to this passage, how should we use the resources God has given us?

How does a strong family create a strong church, which then helps fuel strong communities and a strong society economically?

God has set up His covenant structures to benefit and support each other. He intends every blessing He gives Christians to result in blessings to others. If the Lord has blessed us with more money than we need, it's not so that we can buy bigger houses, fancier cars, and nicer things. God blesses some more than others so they can meet the needs of those who don't have as much. The church should be a place where Christ followers bring their possessions, money, time, and skills to bless others. When the church fulfills this calling, our communities will notice, and God will get the glory.

68

What are some ways the government has or is fulfilling responsibilities that right belong to the family and the church?

What are the church and the family missing out on when they fail to leverage their economic resources to help our culture at large?

When our government and political systems take the place of the church, the church may miss out on God's promise to make us a blessing to others. Even so, individual Christians and families must evaluate their economic plans, principles, and views on politics to make sure they align with God's kingdom.

How do your thoughts about family need to be adjusted as a result of this study?

What are some ways your family can make be a blessing to our wider society?

Closing

As we close out this first session, spend some time praying about the state of families in our nation. Ask God for wisdom on how you can be an instrument and voice for change in strengthening families, churches, and our culture. Take a moment to assess your own contributions to society and in what ways you are allowing God to use you to help others. Identify any changes you need to make and are willing to make.

Bible Study 2
TRUE RELIGION

The church is God's Plan A to reveal His glory and extend His kingdom rule in this world. And while this doesn't intersect with politics directly, it does show up in how a church is to disciple believers on the subject and in the way the church is to assist in community development and support. When churches are strong, the government does not have a vacuum to fill, which can lead to overstepping its reach in society. One of God's values for society rests in the church's ability to carry out her mission of outreach well.

Churches and individual Christians must intentionally and strategically find ways to reach out to their communities. We must willingly sacrifice our time, money, and skills for the benefit of others. And, like Christ, the church must meet both the spiritual and social needs of our society.

When churches begin to look outward and extend their influence beyond the lives of church members, they will make an eternal impact on the broader community where they live. People will be able to see the true religion that pleases God and transforms society.

> *"Pure and undefiled religion in the sight of our God
> and Father is this: to visit orphans and widows in their
> distress, and to keep oneself unstained by the world"*
> JAMES 1:27

How does this verse define what God cares about?

On a scale of 1-10 (with 10 being the most), where would you rate your church's current role of carrying out the mission set forth in James 1:27 as well as Micah 6:8.

0   1   2   3   4   5   6   7   8   9   10

What contributes to the number you chose?

When culture is in disarray, people often respond in one of two ways. They are called *isolationists* and *conformists*. Isolationists try to distance themselves from culture and from the unbelievers on the "sinking ship." Isolationists tend to preach at society instead of engaging society. They focus on doctrine and biblical precision but don't take the time to help people outside the church apply doctrine and biblical truth to their lives.

What are some traits that would describe an isolationist?

Read Romans 12:17-21. How can this passage address isolationism?

Why should your church avoid an isolationist posture?

Conformists look, talk, and act just like nonbelievers. Conformists refuse to tell them that the ship is sinking for fear of offending them. Conformists tend to get so entangled in the culture that they even forget that the ship is going down and that they have the only lifeboat.

What are some traits that describe a conformist?

Read Romans 12:2. What does this verse say about the Christian's relationship with culture?

Why should your church avoid a conformist position?

In the Sermon on the Mount, Jesus explained how the church should live and engage the culture. First, He called us to be salt (Matthew 5:13). One of the characteristics of salt is that it preserves.

While societies around the world decay and crumble under the weight of immorality, violence, and greed, Christians must preserve society. Just as salt extends the life of food, the way Christians love, serve, and extend grace to others should give non-believers a taste of eternal life. Salt can only do its preserving work when someone shakes it on food, and the church can only slow the decaying effects of sin if it gets out into the world.

Reread Matthew 5:13. Who is Jesus addressing in this verse?

How can you display the preserving influence of salt as a church in the area of kingdom politics?

Not only did Jesus tell the church to live as salt in the world, but He also intends to shine His light through the church. One thing light does is drive back the darkness. When you shine a flashlight in a dark corner, the darkness flees. But if you don't turn your flashlight on, the corner remains dark. Jesus entrusted the church with His light—a light that brings life, hope, and clarity. But if the church refuses to shine in the dark places in the world, how will the darkness be dispelled?

Read Ephesians 5:8. Reflect on this verse and put it into your own words.

How has your church shined Christ's light into any dark places? How has your church shined light in areas of politics? Describe those experiences.

Whether or not God creates the chaos in society, He intends the church to be the solution under His divine leading and rule. The church should be on the front line of the battle, bringing the value of the kingdom to bear on the culture

Does your church address the needs of its community? If so, how? If not, what are some ways you can do so?

Does your church partner with neighborhood schools to affect positive social change? If so, how? If not, what are some ways you can do so?

When was the last time you reached out to a neighbor to be a light for Christ?

Closing

Pray right now and ask Jesus to help you and your church live as salt and light in the community. Ask the Holy Spirit to shift the focus from what is wrong in the nation to what you can do to make things right. Then, get to work on it.

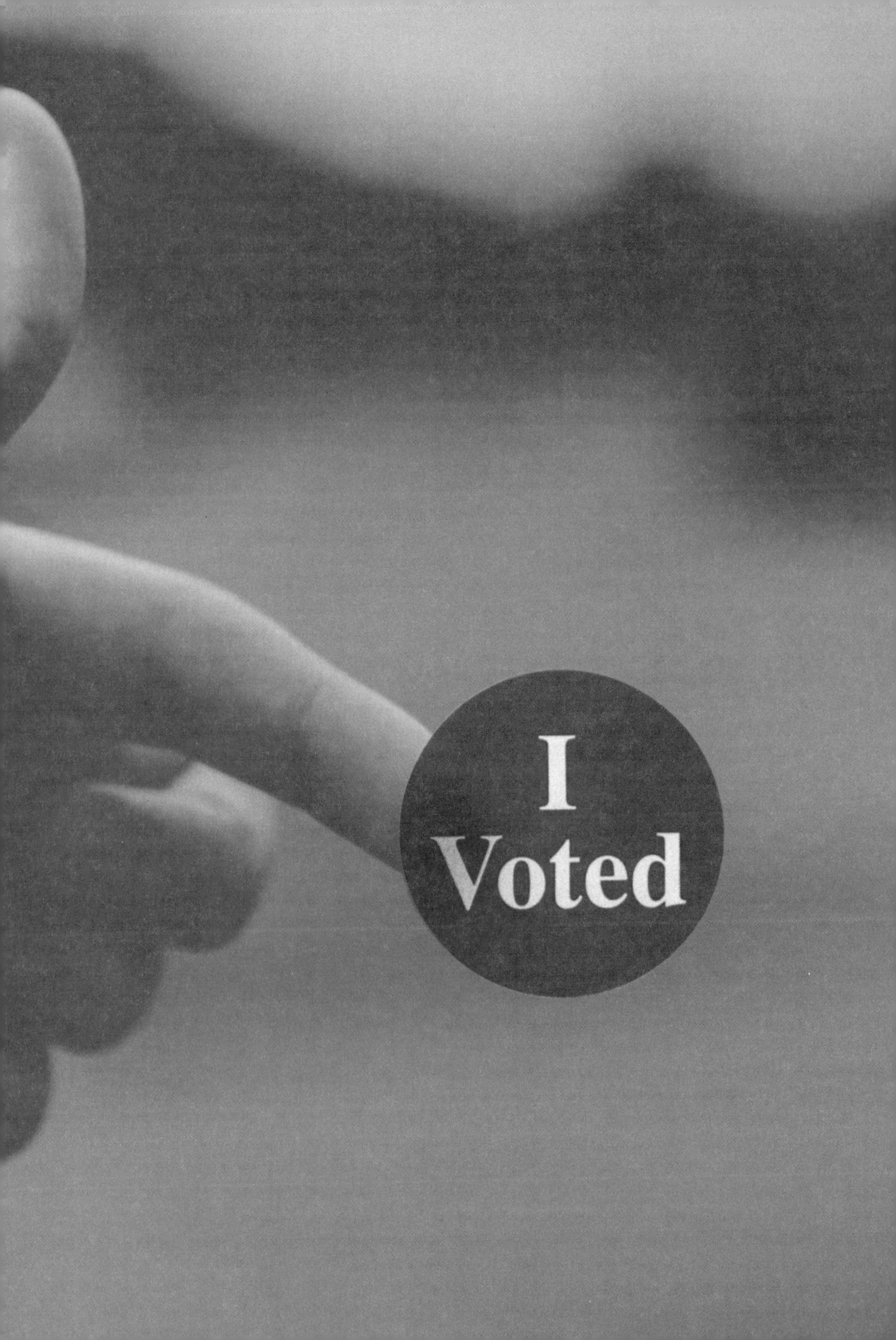
I
Voted

Week 5

THE RESPONSIBILITY OF KINGDOM CITIZENS

Start

Welcome to group session 5.

Last week we examined the priorities that should shape a kingdom citizen's political concerns. This week we will see how our concerns lead to responsibility.

What are some of the primary responsibilities of a kingdom citizen?

Why is it important to engage in the political process in our nation through voting and other means?

The Bible may not be a book about politics, but it talks a lot about the political realm. In the beginning, God set apart Israel to be a nation with no king but God. But Israel rejected God's rule and opted for a human king (1 Samuel 8:7). From then on, human beings have struggled to create moral governments that only fulfill their proper roles. Unfortunately, we have not succeeded in America.

Part of the reason we have not succeeded is the church's failure to disciple believers on how to vote according to their conscience. Many Christians begin with the wrong question of who they should vote for rather than the more important question of how they should vote. Asking the correct question is fundamental to knowing how to arrive at the correct answer.

Kingdom voting is the opportunity and responsibility of committed Christians to partner with God by expanding His rule in society through civil government. Voting is your foundational opportunity to engage in politics in a meaningful way; it is your partnership in the political process.

All through the Bible, God called on people to partner with Him. Scripture makes it clear that we are workers together with God (2 Corinthians 6:1). So, while we must pray for God to bring healing to our land, we must also partner with God for this healing to take place.

Invite someone to pray, then watch the video teaching.

Watch

Use this space to take notes as you watch video session 5.

Discuss

Use the following questions to discuss the video teaching.

When you exercise your right to vote, what are the priorities that shape your vote?

The central theme of the Bible is the glory of God through the expansion of His kingdom. God is king. He is running a kingdom that involves the nations. And He has established the world in such a way to give you the opportunity and responsibility to participate in the process of how He runs it. You participate, at a minimum, through your vote. If you are a Christian and you name the name of Jesus Christ, you don't get to leave God out of your vote. Nor do you just get to vote how you want to vote. You only get to vote for God's glory and the expansion of His kingdom. Your vote should seek to expand God's kingdom rule on earth.

While we stood huddled underneath the overhang of a patio area waiting for a gap in the storm, I prayed. I asked God to clear the weather for us to continue. He did clear it enough for us to make the long walk down to the lake. But shortly after getting to the lake, it started up again. But that is an important lesson in prayer. Prayer doesn't mean we dictate to God what He is to do. Prayer is an action of aligning your heart and mind with God's will. God is not a vending machine where you insert some coins, push a few buttons and get what you want.

What is the relationship between being a responsible Christian and voting?

What influence do we give up we if we refuse to participate in the political process? Why is this important even when the polls don't go the way we hoped?

The God of the Bible does not ride the backs of donkeys or elephants. The God of the Bible is His own independent. He only votes for Himself. There is no political party that only votes God's way. Some represent God's priorities on certain things but do not on others and vice versa. We pick and choose based on our own personal histories and priorities and our conscience and how God is guiding us at that time. Regardless, at your core, you must only view yourself primarily as a kingdom independent since your commitment will be to the kingdom of God over the politics of men.

How would you define a "kingdom independent"?

What does it look like to extend grace and understanding to brothers and sisters whose conscience led them to vote differently than yours?

What do we sacrifice when we allow the church to become divided over political concerns above kingdom concerns?

We are to represent heaven according to our conscience before the Lord. Not everyone's conscience will have the same development or maturity, which is why love, grace, and withholding judgment are so important in the area of politics. Some people value policy over personality or character. Others value personal character over policy. Some desire expanded government while others push for limited government.

Whatever the case, one thing remains the same, we are instructed in Scripture to remain true to what we believe without judging others (Romans 14:1). We are to honor our own conscience while trusting God with the ultimate decisions.

Read Proverbs 16:33. What perspective should verses like this give us as we vote?

Let's close our session this week in prayer.

Prayer

Lord, help me to grow and mature in my understanding of Your Word so that I can participate in the political experience in a way that brings good. Also please help me not to judge others who view things differently than me, knowing You know their hearts and where they are on the growth journey, and You love them too.

Hit the Streets
PRAYER IN THE BALLOT BOX

Prayer is an important part of political influence. The great thing about prayer is that anyone can do it at any time. God has given us multiple examples in Scripture of how prayer can change people's hearts. While you may not be inclined to participating in politics in other ways, there is no reason not to pray. Every believer can pray for our leaders, elections, policies, and the general climate of politics in our nation.

In this week's "Hit the Streets" we are taking things inside to impact the streets, neighborhoods, and cities. Yet while prayer is internal, it is something you can do inside of you wherever you are. Whether you are working, shopping, driving, or any other thing, you can pray. Here are three tips to praying well:

1. When possible, journal your prayers. This form of writing out what you have prayed or even writing prayers verbatim helps solidify the thoughts in your mind. It also gives you a record of what you have prayed so that later on, you can see how the Lord responded to your prayers.

2. Clear your schedule of clutter and noise. Doing this will give you more mental margin to pray. One of the enemies' greatest distractions from carrying out God's work is just that—distractions. By keeping us busy and our schedules full, we fail to maximize the internal life of prayer that the Holy Spirit comes alongside us to fulfill. Clearing your schedule and creating space for yourself and prayer is important.

3. Pray about all aspects. Politics is much more than an election. Politics shows up everywhere. When you pray, don't merely pray for politicians or an election. Instead expand your prayers to cover all aspects of the political realm. When you do this, you will also educate yourself on the various ways politics affects our lives.

Prayer is a gift and a tool given to us by God to influence culture. When you use it well, you will be living as a kingdom disciple fulfilling God's will to advance His kingdom agenda on earth. Pray without ceasing, as Paul states, because prayer impacts lives and ushers in good.

Spend a few moments writing out a prayer to God based on the tips you just read.

Bible Study 1
BECOMING A KINGDOM CITIZEN

When non-believers look at our lives and the way God's people love and care for each other, they should get a taste of God's coming kingdom. While war, poverty, prejudice, and oppression mar our world, the church should be a place where peace, sufficiency, love, and freedom reign supreme.

The kingdom-minded church is a group of Spirit-filled people who have trusted that Jesus is the Son of God and that He died in our place and rose from the dead. They seek to make Jesus known to others through all they say and do. After Peter proclaimed that Jesus is the Son of God, Jesus said He would build His church on this foundational theological truth.

Reflect on Colossians 3:12-17. What characteristics of kingdom citizens does this passage describe?

How would the world look different if people lived like this?

Read James 2:1-9. Examine your life. Have you ever showed partiality to someone? What did you hope to accomplish by showing partiality?

What do these passages teach about the kind of people we should be as we enter the voting booth or any other political engagement?

Read Ephesians 4:1-6. Why is it essential for believers to seek and preserve unity even when we have differing political opinions or passions?

God only supports and "votes" for Himself and His agenda. And God's agenda is always an agenda of unity under His kingdom rule. Unity brings glory to God— that's the bottom line. And yet so much of what we see Christians participating in with regard to their political stance or allegiance involves an atmosphere of vitriol and disunity. The cure for the existing polar divides in our nation rests in God alone. Only when we return to Him and prioritize His will and kingdom agenda on earth will we regain what we have lost in the areas of unity and harmony in our nation.

No political party ought to ever hold your entire allegiance because if and when it veers from God's values and God's priorities, you need to remain committed to God. No politician should supersede God's role in your life. And certainly no politician or party should get the worship you are to give to God and God alone. We can define idolatry, as any noun (person, place, thing) that supersedes God's rightful role in your life and your thoughts.

In what ways has the political process in the country become an idol to many?

How can you contribute to making God as the central priority in your life, family, and church?

You and I will get the answers to our nation's issues when we surrender to God Himself. The strategies for our nation's success rest in God. Politicians often don't have to deal with Christians or our voices because Satan has been so strategic at dividing us. We are broken up into groups of people set against each other rather than working together for God and His glory.

Kingdom voters and kingdom-minded citizens understand that they have been given the opportunity and the responsibility to partner with God for the expansion of His rule in society. Kingdom voters and kingdom-minded citizens understand that God is ruler over all. The closer we align with Him through the voice of our votes and participation in society, the greater we will experience His power and His presence in our land.

We'll end our time in this personal study by examining a few verses that give us guidance on how to engage and be productive kingdom citizens.

Read the following Bible verses, summarizing the passages and writing down a personal application action item you learn from each one:

Submit yourselves for the Lord's sake to every human institution, whether to a king as the one in authority, or to governors as sent by him for the punishment of evildoers and the praise of those who do right.
1 PETER 2:13-14

Summary:

Main Action Item:

Furthermore, in your bedroom do not curse a king, and in your sleeping rooms do not curse a rich person; for a bird of the sky will bring the sound, and the winged one will make your word known.
ECCLESIASTES 10:20

Summary:

Main Action Item:

Therefore it is necessary to be in subjection, not only because of wrath, but also for the sake of conscience.
ROMANS 13:5

Summary:

Main Action Item:

Do not speak against one another, brothers and sisters. The one who speaks against a brother or sister, or judges his brother or sister, speaks against the law and judges the law; but if you judge the law, you are not a doer of the law but a judge of it. Do not speak against one another, brethren. He who speaks against a brother or judges his brother, speaks against the law and judges the law; but if you judge the law, you are not a doer of the law but a judge of it.

JAMES 4:11

Summary:

Main Action Item:

Let no unwholesome word come out of your mouth, but if there is any good word for edification according to the need of the moment, say that, so that it will give grace to those who hear.

EPHESIANS 4:29

Summary:

Main Action Item:

Closing

Consider how often you speak or think about political subjects and compare this with how often you speak or think on God and His Word. If there needs to be an adjustment, consider making that adjustment.

Bible Study 2

PUFFED UP

A person's conscience is his or her heart regulator. It is the thing that regulates between right and wrong, good and bad, or up and down. It's like the beeper that goes off when somebody comes into your house while it's locked and the alarm system has been turned on. It lets you know something has gone terribly wrong. It is the light that flashes, begging you to pay attention in order to avoid the terrible calamity the warning signals.

God has built into every human being a conscience that serves to both govern and guide them. If and when the conscience is informed properly, it will do its job. But since the heart is deceitfully wicked, an uninformed or a corrupted conscience will drive a person toward wrong (Jeremiah 17:9). This is why it is critical that everyone's conscience gets the right data to make the wisest possible decisions.

But this isn't the case in every person. We are all influenced by a variety of experiences in our lives that either sharpen or dull our consciences. That's why the Bible tells us in Romans 14:1 that we are to accept those who are weak in faith, and we are not to pass judgment on their opinions.

Read Romans 14:2-6:
> *One person has faith that he may eat all things, but the one who is weak eats only vegetables. The one who eats is not to regard with contempt the one who does not eat, and the one who does not eat is not to judge the one who eats, for God has accepted him. Who are you to judge the servant of another? To his own master he stands or falls; and he will stand, for the Lord is able to make him stand. One person values one day over another, another values every day the same. Each person must be fully convinced in his own mind. The one who observes the day, observes it for the Lord, and the one who eats, does so with regard to the Lord, for he gives thanks to God; and the one who does not eat, it is for the Lord that he does not eat, and he gives thanks to God.*
> ROMANS 14:2-6

What are some of the things (actions) in contemporary society that we can replace "vegetables" and "observances" in this passage with?

Why is it important to allow other people the grace to be where they are on their own spiritual growth journey?

How can judging others (or being judged by others) hinder someone's spiritual development?

What are some ways we can disciple and help others develop their conscience without judging?

What are some ways Christians "judge" others regarding politics? In what ways can this be harmful?

When people's political affiliations cause them to reject, demean, ridicule, curse, or avoid those who differ from them based on their conscience before God, they are violating this passage. We are each on a different plane of advancement and growth. If you were to look at your life in retrospect, I am sure there are things you believed years ago that you don't now—or vice versa. As we all grow in the Lord, truth and the prioritization of that truth manifests itself differently in our lives. The better path than judgment is grace-based and kingdom-minded discipleship that happens in relationships.

The saying goes, "You can catch more flies with honey than with vinegar." What does this saying mean to you?

How can the meaning of this saying apply to winning people over to God's kingdom values regarding our nation and politics?

Read Matthew 12:25. Why is it important to maintain unity and keep the peace in the body of Christ?

Everyone in the body of Christ may not feel the same about democrats or republicans, or this candidate as opposed to the other candidate, but those differences are not to get in the way of our fellowship. They are not to get in the way of our service together in advancing God's kingdom on earth. As followers of Jesus Christ, we ought to talk to each other respectfully even if we disagree politically. We must recognize the fact that there are good and bad people and policies on both sides of the political divide.

Read 1 Corinthians 4:6. What are the dangers of becoming arrogant in your views? Why would Paul warn against it?

Take a moment to write out five reasons why respect in communication and withholding judgment are important values in the body of Christ.

Reason One:

Reason Two:

Reason Three:

Reason Four:

Reason Five:

It's not wrong to disagree. It's not wrong to vote differently than another believer. It is wrong to be contemptuous in both. Kingdom-minded people accept other kingdom-minded people regardless of political affiliation. We accept each other because God accepts both of us. So, when you attack other people in the family of God because they believe, think, act, or vote differently than you, you have attacked God. This is no small thing. The division of our nation down racial, political, class, and even conspiratorial lines is straight from Satan's playbook. A person's mouth reflects his or her heart. If people's mouths spew vitriol at those who disagree with their political affiliations, then neither their mouths nor their hearts are aligned with God.

Closing

Let's close this session in prayer. Jesus, please unify Your followers in our hearts. Even though we may disagree on certain areas, help us to always show respect to each other. Help each of us to vote our conscience before You and not to judge others who may disagree with us. Raise up Your body to have a lasting impact for good on our nation.

Week 6

THE STRATEGY FOR KINGDOM TRANSFORMATION

Start

Welcome to group session 6.

We've come to our final session on this all-important subject of kingdom politics. As a reminder, kingdom politics involves believers' active engagement in influencing and engaging in that which governs our nation, whether through voting or otherwise.

What are some of your favorite insights from this study so far?

How can a concerted effort by believers to infuse God's standards into our nation help improve the overall climate of our culture?

Unfortunately, the digression of influence in our culture is largely due to the failure of Christians and the church to remain actively engaged and relevant. As citizens first and foremost of God's kingdom, how should Christians respond when the government seeks to overstep God's authority? How should Christians try to reform political systems? Kingdom political involvement recognizes that since God rules over all, the political realm must be held accountable for straying from His authority and brought back into submission to Him.

How should we work to bring the government back under the Lord's authority? We certainly shouldn't use illegitimate means to force change at the top levels of the government. Instead, we should work toward spiritual transformation in individual lives and in our communities. Christians should also exercise their rights to vote and voice their biblical values in local, state, and national government policies.

Invite someone to pray, then watch the video teaching.

Watch

Use this space to take notes as you watch video session 6.

Discuss

Use the following questions to discuss the video teaching.

Our nation has been infiltrated by destructive thought-forms. We have secularism, humanism, and all forms of idolatry. Yet we need to keep in mind that God has not called His people to sit on the sidelines of this battle. He has called each of us to step up and get involved in proactive and helpful ways.

What is one way a church can get involved to influence culture and politics in a helpful, proactive manner?

Why should the church take influencing policies and politics seriously?

Looking at the political landscape, we can't help but long for a time when peace and justice will rule. Our government has either enacted policies that favor racism and the slaughter of the unborn, or it has allowed the dehumanization of individuals with special needs and the abandonment of the elderly when they are no longer "productive citizens." Ungodly policies like these make us long for the return of Christ. But until His return, we need to be actively engaged in influencing our nation for good.

Read Psalm 128:5-6 together. How does our involvement in kingdom building work extend beyond us?

When individual Christians and the church as a whole fulfill their roles to inject God's standards into the political sphere, peace will characterize our land. In the Bible, the word for peace is *shalom*. Shalom is a sense of wholeness and well-being in the community. Shalom comes as a result of righteousness because of right relationships with God and others. When shalom takes over, prosperity increases and spiritual health characterizes the community.

Describe how a presence of shalom, or peace, leads to a more prosperous nation?

What benefits can come to the world on behalf of the gospel when a nation is prosperous?

In America, violence and spiritual unrest has snuffed out shalom. We must transform our culture from the bottom up, starting with our individual lives, families, and churches. It's up to us to step up and get involved. Christians must exercise their rights and speak against wicked ideas before they become laws and policies. The only way our nation can experience peace and blessing is by implementing God's definition of government through an influence of kingdom politics.

How can the church act as a prophetic voice to the government?

How can the government protect the church's freedom to exercise this role?

The church should serve as a prophet to the government and the culture, explaining how God's Word applies to the political realm. The church should demonstrate God's priorities and His love for the outcasts of society by placing itself between godless policies and the innocent.

Does your church help its members to develop a divine perspective on government and train them to stand up for godly policies in the public square? Explain.

Do you consider yourself an engaged citizen or apathetic? Why?

What is one principle from this study you will put into practice?

Christians must pray for their local, state, and national government leaders. We must seek to be kingdom-minded participants who are involved in the political realm in order to lead our selves and our nation to love God and serve others.

Let's close our session this week in prayer.

Prayer

Lord, raise up Your kingdom followers to influence our
nation for Your glory and the greater good of humanity.

Hit the Streets
KINGDOM TRANSFORMATION STRATEGY

The urgent need today is for churches to become discipleship training centers for developing their members to become kingdom disciples who learn to progressively bring all of life under the lordship of Jesus Christ (Matthew 28:18-20). The church is God's authorized kingdom agency that has been given divine authority—"the keys of the kingdom of heaven"—to exercise kingdom authority on God's behalf in history (Matthew 16:18-19).

The kingdom-minded church must accept the responsibility and challenge of leading the way in reversing our political divides since we, to a large degree, are responsible in helping to keep it enflamed. Here is a three-step plan to pursue transformational change in our nation. Commit to studying this plan and discussing how to implement it as a group:

1. ASSEMBLE: UNIFIED SACRED GATHERING. The problem is not just our waiting on God to involve Himself in our country's demise but that God is waiting on us to call on Him collectively, according to His prescribed manner. Kingdom-minded leaders should develop a community-wide fellowship that meets regularly and hosts an annual solemn assembly (Isaiah 58:1-12; Ephesians 2:11-22).

2. ADDRESS: UNIFIED COMPASSIONATE VOICE. It is time to set our platforms and personal agendas aside when it comes to matters of national importance so that we can effectively speak into and address the concerns of our day. Kingdom-minded leaders should actively develop disciples who speak out with unified messaging, offering biblical truths and solutions on contemporary cultural issues (Matthew 28:16–20; John 17:13-23).

3. ACT: UNIFIED SOCIAL IMPACT. We will make a bigger impact when we intentionally align our actions to produce greater momentum. Kingdom-minded leaders collectively mobilize their churches, small groups, communities, or organizations to carry out a visible presence of ongoing good works improving the well-being of underserved communities (Jeremiah 29:5-7; Matthew 5:13-16).

How can you implement these steps in your life?

Your family?

Your church?

This is a defining moment for us as churches and citizens to decide whether we want to be one nation under God or a divided nation apart from God. If we don't answer that question correctly, and if we don't answer it quickly, we won't be much of a nation at all (2 Chronicles 15:3-6; Psalm 33:12).

Bible Study 1
STAND UP AND GET INVOLVED

There are several ways Christians can get involved when governments are not functioning entirely by God's divine standards. One of these ways is called "interposition." Interposition means to place ourselves between two parties to intervene. It allows us to stand up and get involved.

Read Genesis 18:16-33. How did Abraham interpose himself between God and the destruction of Sodom and Gomorrah?

How can prayer make a tangible difference in our national affairs?

We can interpose ourselves between the ungodly policies and those who are being unjustly treated. We can do this physically by voting for those who uphold biblical values, taking part in peaceful protests, or contacting our representatives.

We can also do this spiritually through intercessory prayer. When God wanted to judge the evil citizens of Sodom and Gomorrah, Abraham begged God to relent if He found ten righteous people in the land. And God listened. Likewise, Christians should pray for God's grace on our nation and that He would protect anyone disenfranchised by unjust policies or programs.

Read Exodus 32:1-14. How did Moses interpose himself between God and His idolatrous people? What was the result?

Read Esther 4:1-7. How did Esther risk her life to stop the wicked plans of her government to exterminate her people? What was the result?

How can you apply this principle of interposition in your life? Are you an informed, involved citizen? Why or why not?

When the laws of the land directly violate God's standard of right and wrong, Christians must resist those laws. But we must also respect our government because it has received its authority from God. So how do we harmonize these seemingly opposing principles? History has given us some good examples of Christians who risked their lives to stand up to evil government policies and protect the innocent.

During the Holocaust when the Nazis systematically killed Jews, Corrie ten Boom and her family hid Jews in a secret room in their house. When Martin Luther King Jr. saw the blatant racism in our national policies, he organized a non-violent movement that changed the laws and transformed our nation.

Today, our law allows people to murder the unborn in the name of convenience, and Christians must interpose themselves between this abhorrent policy and the innocent victims. But no matter how passionate we feel about this and other issues, we must not use force or violence to make a point. We should find peaceful ways to stand up for God's standard and protect the defenseless.

Read Matthew 5:9. How can Christians practice interposition and be peacemakers at the same time?

Read Exodus 1:15-22. How did the Hebrew midwives practice interposition? What was the result? How can we apply this example in our lives today?

This is a time to lovingly and responsibly take our stand for the lordship of Jesus Christ. This is our time to bring the values of heaven to bear on earth. That's why we are here. God didn't leave us here to sit, sulk, and sour. He didn't leave us here just to go to church on Sunday either. He left us here to penetrate the culture with the customs of heaven.

What might it look like for you to implement interposition as a part of the kingdom transformation strategy? What might this look like in unified sacred gathering of kingdom citizens?

Unfortunately, we have become a platform of divided parties rather than a unified sacred body of believers. We won't ask anyone to explain what Scripture has to say. And we are suffering the results of this spiritual exclusion from politics. Unity in prayer keeps us from drifting into the wisdom of the world.

James 3 calls God's thoughts wisdom from above. But in this passage, he also points out that there is "earthly wisdom" too. It is wisdom that comes from demons.

Read James 3:13-18:

> *Who among you is wise and understanding? Let him show by his good behavior his deeds in the gentleness of wisdom. But if you have bitter jealousy and selfish ambition in your heart, do not be arrogant and so lie against the truth. This wisdom is not that which comes down from above, but is earthly, natural, demonic. For where jealousy and selfish ambition exist, there is disorder and every evil thing. But the wisdom from above is first pure, then peace-loving, gentle, reasonable, full of mercy and good fruits, impartial, free of hypocrisy. And the fruit of righteousness is sown in peace by those who make peace.*
>
> JAMES 3:13-18

Describe earthly wisdom in your own terms.

How does this show up in political discourse?

Describe God's wisdom in your own terms.

How could this positively impact political discourse?

"Earthly wisdom" is actually demonic thought. Whenever what you think, say, or hear disagrees with what God says on the subject, you have just taken sides with demons. You have become demonized. Because of this, we have a lot of demonized Christians walking around talking about politics, policies, and priorities emphasizing the world's standards instead of God's. In essence, they have joined the cohorts of earthlings. It's harsh language, but it is rooted in Scripture. Satan seeks to soften his strategy by painting "earthly wisdom" as beneficial or tolerant.

How might a unified church make a stand against worldly wisdom that plagues us?

What would change if the church implemented the second step in the kingdom transformation strategy and spoke with a unified compassionate voice?

Closing

As we close this section, ask God to shape our political discourse and involvement as believers so that we bear fruit for His glory. Ask the Holy Spirit to pour out divine wisdom on all who follow the Lord Jesus Christ so that our nation may benefit.

Bible Study 2
IN THE WORLD, NOT OF THE WORLD

Governments are divinely created systems wherein God entrusts the care of people to the rule of leaders. When they are aligned underneath His standards, the nation runs smoothly and the inhabitants benefit. But when they are not aligned under God's standards, chaos can ensue. God is our rightful King and His rules are aimed to protect us and provide for us. However, humanity has often sought leadership outside of God's rule. For example, Israel asked for a king in addition to God.

God wanted to save Israel from having a human king who, as he grew in power and pride, would overstep his legitimate boundaries and begin to encroach on the freedom of his citizens. But Israel wanted to have a human king like all their neighboring nations, so they rejected God as their sole king. Samuel warned Israel about the possibility that their future king's government would grow too big and would require more than they wanted to pay (1 Samuel 8:10-18).

Read Psalm 24:1. How can we worship God as the Lord of everything and still obey the government?

How should we respond when the government oversteps its boundaries?

What are a few ways you feel like the government has overstepped?

What is a way the church can make a unified impact (step three of the kingdom transformation strategy) when this happens?

When Jesus stood before Pilate, Jesus reminded Pilate that his authority to sentence Jesus came from God. All governmental authority has been given by God. Sadly, many elected officials want to expand the government and encroach on citizens' responsibilities to God, family, and church. Even so, Jesus affirmed our responsibility to pay taxes. But everything we have belongs to God; therefore, we should give to God the firstfruits of our time, talents, and treasures before taxes.

Read 2 Corinthians 9:1-15. Since everything we have belongs to God, how does that change the way we should view giving our resources?

How does generously giving our resources keep us from becoming too tied to the world?

We are to be in the world but not of the world. Our loyalty is not here. Until we satisfy the issue of the lordship of Jesus Christ and our allegiance to Him and His rule, our nation will continue to crumble. When we follow Jesus as Lord, we actively advance His kingdom and His kingdom values throughout all we do and say. This isn't done violently or forcibly, but neither is it done passively. We are to be consistent in the promotion of kingdom values throughout the land. We are to do it with love but we are to do it. Love doesn't mean we agree with everyone on everything. Love means we promote truth, righteousness, and justice in every opportunity we can while challenging our political leaders to do the same.

A very common wartime strategy is that known as the "Fifth Column." When a country deploys a fifth columnist approach to war, they seek to infiltrate the culture to influence it in the way they want. They send people into the opposing country to assimilate and become doctors, educators, politicians, businesspeople, judges, and more. In this way, they can destroy the opposing country from within. It turns into a strategy of sabotage. Sometimes this sabotage takes place prior to a larger invasion. But other times, it is enough on its own to deflate a nation of its resources and make it vulnerable enough for a quick and easy defeat.

Jesus has sent us into this world prior to His return to set up His kingdom agenda in all areas of life, including the political realm. Remember, Jesus is always on the ballot. We are to be His fifth columnists who have been sent in to set things up for the big invasion of His earthly kingdom called "His Millennial Reign." We are to influence culture in every capacity so that the values of the kingdom of God become the dominant values in the land. We are to take our stand in society so that we set up the return of the one true King. That's what living as a kingdom citizen means. We emphasize and promote God's values in a world that seeks to leave Him out.

As a kingdom citizen, your allegiance is to God and your vote or voice must be clear. There is no undecided voter when it comes to living as a Christian. Depending on what the issue is, you need to take your stand for Him.

What are some ways you can take your stand for God in our nation?

Why do you think it's so important for believers to unify under God and dissolve the divisions political leaders, news channels and others seek to create?

The trajectory of our nation can be reversed. Kingdom citizens can influence police-community relations, policies, healthcare reform, and more. We do it through standing up as citizens of heaven while drawing down God's viewpoint into earth's decisions. In all we do, we need to represent God first.

We must understand that politics doesn't bring salvation. No savior will show up in the political realm. If God is not postured properly in the hearts and minds of a nation's citizens, it doesn't matter who is elected to lead. The more secular a country becomes, the less of God that country will see. The less of God that is seen, the more chaos will ensue. Thus, the church better shake itself up, wake up, and get up so that we can see what God can do when people commit their lives to Him as citizens of His kingdom, honoring Him as King.

To end this study take what you've learned and write your own Kingdom Transformation Strategy using the steps Dr. Evans supplied (pages 96-97).

1. ASSEMBLE: Unified Sacred Gathering.

2. ADDRESS: Unified Compassionate Voice.

3. ACT: Unified Social Impact.

Closing

Let's close our time together in this Bible study with prayer.
Pray as you feel led to ask the Holy Spirit's power to develop
and mature you and the small group you participated
in this study with to impact our nation for God.

The key to spiritual victory is not based on your strength but your surrender.

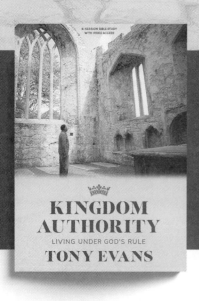

RISE

UP

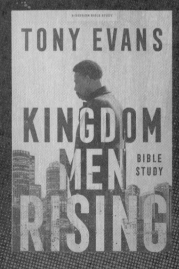

YOUR *Eternity* IS OUR *Priority*

At The Urban Alternative, eternity is our priority—for the individual, the family, the church and the nation. The 45-year teaching ministry of Tony Evans has allowed us to reach a world in need with:

The Alternative – Our flagship radio program brings hope and comfort to an audience of millions on over 1,300 radio outlets across the country.

tonyevans.org – Our library of teaching resources provides solid Bible teaching through the inspirational books and sermons of Tony Evans.

Tony Evans Training Center – Experience the adventure of God's Word with our online classroom, providing at-your-own-pace courses for your PC or mobile device.

Tony Evans app – Packed with audio and video clips, devotionals, Scripture readings and dozens of other tools, the mobile app provides inspiration on-the-go.

**Explore God's kingdom today.
Live for more than the moment.
Live for** *eternity.*

tonyevans.org

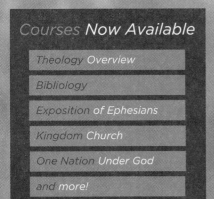

Politics divide. Christ unites.

In this study, Tony Evans covers the foundational Bible principles for integrating politics into our daily lives. He challenges readers to incorporate all of Scripture when addressing divisive issues.

ADDITIONAL RESOURCES

eBOOK
Bible Study eBook with Video Access

005847288 **$19.99**

DVD Set

005847299 **$29.99**

Price and availability subject to change without notice.

When you understand the purpose of government from a kingdom perspective, you can maintain your political affiliations without causing divisions in your church or family, and you can take sides on moral issues while demonstrating the compassion and love of Jesus Christ.

- Learn the biblical principles that form the basis of every human government.

- Confirm the types of issues that Christians should concern themselves with in the political arena.

- See how to engage and be active on issues that matter the most.

Studying on your own?
To enrich your study experience, be sure to access the videos available through a redemption code printed in this Bible Study Book.

Leading a group?
Each group member will need a Kingdom Politics Bible Study Book, which includes video access. This gives participants complete access to the video content individually.

Kingdom
POLITICS

GOVERNMENT *from*
GOD'S PERSPECTIVE

TONY EVANS

Here's Your Video Access

To stream the Bible study teaching videos, follow these steps:

1. Go to my.lifeway.com/redeem and register or log in to your Lifeway account.

2. Enter this redemption code to gain access to your individual-use video license:

X L Z G R B W 5 D 8 B 2

Once you've entered your personal redemption code, you can stream the Bible study teaching videos any time from your Digital Media page on my.lifeway.com or watch them via the Lifeway On Demand app on a compatible TV or mobile device via your Lifeway account.

There's no need to enter your code more than once!
To watch your streaming videos, just log in to your Lifeway account at my.lifeway.com or watch using the Lifeway On Demand app.

QUESTIONS? WE HAVE ANSWERS!
Visit support.lifeway.com and search "Video Redemption Code" or "Video Streaming FAQ" or call our Tech Support Team at 866.627.8553.